NETWORKS

IN THE MEADOW

John McInnes, *Senior Author*

John Ryckman

NELSON CANADA

© Nelson Canada,
A Division of International Thomson Limited, 1986

All rights in this book are reserved

Published in 1986 by
Nelson Canada,
A Division of International Thomson Limited
1120 Birchmount Road
Scarborough, Ontario
M1K 5G4

ISBN 0-17-602351-8

Canadian Cataloguing in Publication Data

McInnes, John, 1927-
   In the Meadow

(Networks)

ISBN 0-17-602351-8

1. Readers (Elementary). I. Ryckman, John, 1928-
II. Title. III. Series: Networks (Toronto, Ont.)

PE1119.M2536 1986   428.6   C85-099869-7

Contents

Houses Have Faces

Houses have faces.
Some houses look sad.
Their window-eyes cry.
Their front doors
Seem to say
"Nobody lives here."

Houses have faces.
Some houses smile.
Their window-eyes twinkle.
Their front doors
Seem to say
"Welcome!"

The House Where Nobody Lives

The old house stood
at the side of the road.
The front door was boarded up.
The shutters on the windows were closed,
and tall grass grew all around.

Every day the school bus
passed the old house,
and the children said,
"There's the house where nobody lives."

Every day the bus driver said,
"You're right.
But we don't stop here.
We don't stop at houses
where nobody lives."

One day one of the children said,
"Look at the house where nobody lives!
The front door is open."

"You're right," said the bus driver.
"But nobody lives there yet.
We don't stop at houses
where nobody lives."

The next day one of the childen said,
"Look at the house where nobody lives!
The shutters are open
and the grass is cut."

"You're right," said the bus driver.
"But nobody lives there yet.
We don't stop at houses
where nobody lives."

The next day one of the children said,
"Look at the house where nobody lives!
There's a little boy coming out
the front door."

"You're right," said the bus driver.
"Somebody lives there now."

She stopped the bus
and opened the door.

The boy ran to the bus
and got on.

"Welcome aboard," said the bus driver.
"Boys and girls, this is Bobby Gray.
From now on the bus stops
at this house every day!"

My Name Is Bobby G.

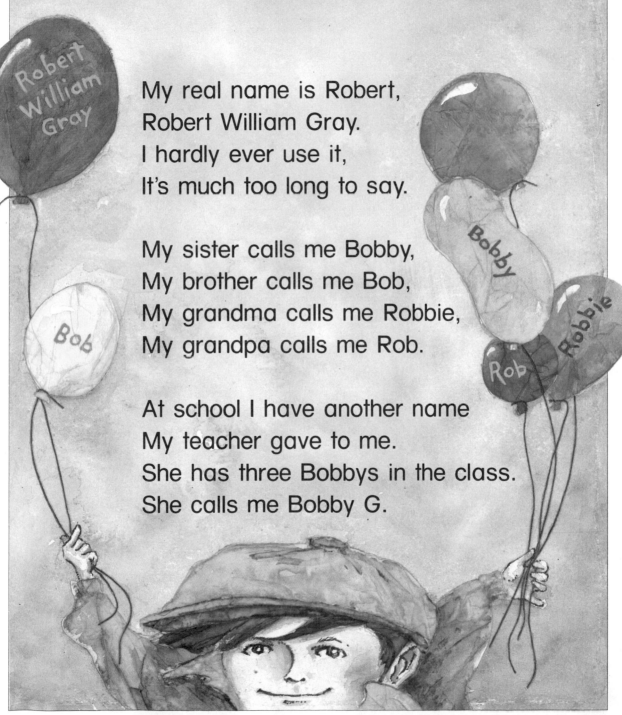

My real name is Robert,
Robert William Gray.
I hardly ever use it,
It's much too long to say.

My sister calls me Bobby,
My brother calls me Bob,
My grandma calls me Robbie,
My grandpa calls me Rob.

At school I have another name
My teacher gave to me.
She has three Bobbys in the class.
She calls me Bobby G.

Hurry Up!

Every morning on their way to school,
the children passed Anna's house.
Anna was always waiting for them
at the gate.

One morning Anna wasn't there.

"Where's Anna?" asked Penny.
"She's always waiting for us."

"Maybe she's sick in bed,"
said Vito.

Just then, Anna came out the door.

"Hurry up, Anna," the children called.
"Run! Run!"

But Anna didn't run.
She walked very, very slowly.
She was carrying something in a jar.

Penny called, "Come on, Anna!
Hurry up!"

"I can't hurry up," said Anna.
"I'm walking as fast as I can."

At last Anna got to the gate.

"Why were you walking so slowly?"
asked Vito.

"Because," said Anna,
"I have a caterpillar in a jar.
And caterpillars always walk slowly."

Everybody laughed.

The Marvellous Caterpillar

Anna showed the caterpillar
to her friends.

"Look at it go!" said Marty.

"It must have ten legs!" said Vito.

"It has more legs than that,"
said Penny.
"I bet it has a hundred!"

"I know what," said Marty.
"Let's pretend we're a caterpillar!"

"Great!" said all the children.

Mrs. Hill was waiting
at the school door.
She saw the children coming.
"What are you doing?"
she asked.

"We're a caterpillar," said Anna.
"This is how caterpillars walk."

Mrs. Hill laughed.

Anna showed the caterpillar to Mrs. Hill.
Mrs. Hill looked at it in the jar.

"What a marvellous caterpillar!" she said.
"Let's take a closer look at it.
We can use a magnifying glass."

Everyone took turns
looking at the caterpillar.

Vito asked, "Can we keep the caterpillar?"

"Yes," said Mrs. Hill.
"I'll help you make a house for it."

The children looked
at the caterpillar every day.
They took turns
using the magnifying glass.
They took turns
feeding the caterpillar.
They gave it a name.
They called the caterpillar "Speedy."

The Magnifying Glass

This is a magnifying glass.
It makes things look bigger.

Look at your finger
without a magnifying glass.

Now look at your finger
with a magnifying glass.

What did you see
that you didn't see before?

Look at a leaf
without a magnifying glass.

Now look at the leaf
with a magnifying glass.

What did you see
that you didn't see before?

Look at a piece of wool
without a magnifying glass.

Now look at the wool
with a magnifying glass.

What did you see
that you didn't see before?

Call Me Speedy

My name is Speedy.
I'm soft and I'm furry.
I walk very slowly,
Even when I'm in a hurry.

Marvellous, marvellous,
Marvellous me.
There's nobody else
That I'd rather be!

I creep and I crawl
In the grass on the ground.
I stretch myself tall
And I look all around.

I love eating breakfast,
Dinner, and lunch.
Wherever I go,
I find something to munch.

Marvellous, marvellous,
Marvellous me.
There's nobody else
That I'd rather be...
Except maybe a butterfly!

The Big Race

Part One: Ready! Set! Go!

Early one morning,
all the animals hurried to the pond.
It was the day of The Big Race.

Rosie climbed up on a big stump.
"Is everybody here?" she called.

"Yes," shouted all the animals.

"Good," said Rosie.
"Listen, and I'll tell you
all about The Big Race."

Rosie said, "Here is a map
of The Big Race.
The race starts at this stump.
It goes around The Honey Tree,
over Strawberry Hill,
across The Swinging Bridge,
past Cozy Cave,
and back to this stump."

All the animals looked at the map.

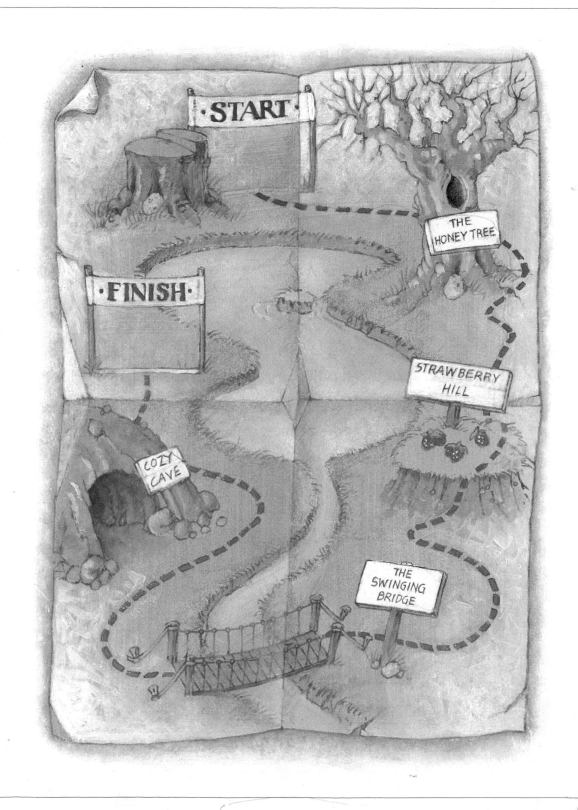

B.J. climbed up on the big stump.
"Listen," he said.
"Here are the rules:
    I start the race.
    Rosie picks the runners.
    Two can run at the same time."

Rosie picked two names
out of a hat.
She read the names.
Then she called,
"The first runners are...
Dragon and Speedy."

"Come on, Speedy," said Dragon.
"We're first."

"Marvellous!" said Speedy.

Dragon and Speedy lined up
at the big stump.

B.J. called, "Ready! Set! Go!"

Dragon and Speedy started off.

Part Two: The Winner

The Big Race was on.
Dragon ran fast.
Speedy crawled along slowly.

Soon Dragon came to The Honey Tree.
"I hear some bees buzzing,"
he said. "I feel hungry.
I'll find myself some honey to eat."
Dragon stopped to look for honey.

Speedy saw Dragon eating honey.
She didn't stop.
Speedy kept right on going.

Dragon started running again.
He ran very fast.
Speedy crawled along slowly.

Soon Dragon came to Strawberry Hill.
"I see some big, red strawberries,"
he said. "I feel hungry again.
I'll pick myself some strawberries to eat."
Dragon stopped to pick strawberries.

Speedy saw Dragon eating strawberries.
She didn't stop.
Speedy kept right on going.

Dragon started running again.
Soon he came to The Swinging Bridge.
He started across the bridge
and it began to swing.
"This is fun," said Dragon.
"I'll stop and swing on the bridge."

Speedy saw Dragon swinging on the bridge.
She didn't stop.
Speedy kept right on going.

Dragon started running again.
Soon he came to Cozy Cave.
He stopped and went in.
"I feel sleepy," he said.
"I'll have myself a little nap."
Dragon fell asleep.

Speedy saw Dragon asleep in the cave.
She didn't stop.
Speedy kept right on going.

It began to get dark.

B.J. said, "I'm going home to bed."

All the other animals said,
"We're going home to bed too."

Rosie said, "You can't go home.
The race isn't over yet.
We have to wait and see who wins."

Just then, they saw Speedy
crawling along slowly.

"Here comes Speedy now!" said B.J.

"Come on, Speedy!" called all the animals.

At last Speedy got to the big stump.

"Hurrah for Speedy!" shouted Rosie.
"Speedy is the winner!"

"That's the way it goes," said B.J.
"Slow and steady wins the race."

"Marvellous me!" said Speedy.

Boris and Morris

by Bernard Wiseman

Boris the Bear met Morris the Moose.
"Do you like riddles?" Boris asked.

Morris asked, "How do they taste?"

Boris said, "You do not eat riddles."

Morris asked, "Do you drink them?"

Boris said, "You do not eat riddles.
You do not drink riddles. You ask them!
Listen—I will ask you a riddle."

Boris asked, "What has four feet..."

Morris yelled, "ME!"

"I did not finish," Boris said.
"What has four feet and a tail..."

"ME!" Morris yelled.

"I still did not finish!" Boris cried.
"Let me finish!"

Morris put a hoof over his mouth.

Boris asked, "What has four feet
and a tail and flies?"

"ME!" Morris yelled.
"I have four feet and a tail,
and flies come and sit on me
all the time!"

"No, no!" Boris growled.
"The answer is:
A horse in an airplane!"

"Here is another riddle.
What kind of comb cannot comb hair?"

"I know!" Morris cried.
"A broken comb!"

"NO! NO! NO!" Boris shouted.
"The answer is: a honeycomb!"

"What is a honeycomb?"
Morris asked.

Boris said, "It is a bee house.
Don't you know anything?"

Morris said, "I know about riddles.
You do not eat riddles.
You do not drink riddles.
You *ask* riddles."

Boris said, "And you must answer them!
Try to answer this riddle.
What kind of bee does not sting?"

"I know!" cried Morris.
"A friendly bee!"

"NO! NO!" Boris yelled.

Morris cried, "A sleeping bee!"

"NO! NO! NO!" Boris shouted.
"The answer is: a beetle.
Oh, you don't know how
to answer riddles.
I am not going to ask you
any more."

Over in the Meadow

Traditional

Over in the meadow,
In the sand, in the sun,
Lived an old mother mouse
And her little mouse one.
"Dance," said the mother.
"I dance," said the one.
So he danced all day
In the sand, in the sun.

Over in the meadow,
Where the waters run blue,
Lived an old mother frog
And her little frogs two.
"Splash," said the mother.
"We splash," said the two.
So they splashed all day
Where the waters run blue.

Over in the meadow,
In the big green tree,
Lived an old mother squirrel
And her little squirrels three.
"Whisper," said the mother.
"We whisper," said the three.
So they whispered all day
In the big green tree.

Over in the meadow,
By the old barn door,
Lived an old mother cat
And her little kittens four.
"Mew," said the mother.
"We mew," said the four.
So they mewed all day
By the old barn door.

Over in the meadow,
In the big beehive,
Lived an old mother bee
And her little bees five.
"Buzz," said the mother.
"We buzz," said the five.
So they buzzed all day
In the big beehive.

Over in the meadow,
In the nest made of sticks,
Lived an old mother robin
And her little robins six.
"Eat," said the mother.
"We eat," said the six.
So they ate all day
In the nest made of sticks.

Over in the meadow,
Where the grass grows even,
Lived an old mother goat
And her little goats seven.
"Run," said the mother.
"We run," said the seven.
So they ran all day
Where the grass grows even.

Over in the meadow,
By the old farm gate,
Lived an old mother rabbit
And her little rabbits eight.
"Jump," said the mother.
"We jump," said the eight.
So they jumped all day
By the old farm gate.

Over in the meadow,
Where the blue waters shine,
Lived an old mother beaver
And her little beavers nine.
"Work," said the mother.
"We work," said the nine.
So they worked all day
Where the blue waters shine.

Over in the meadow,
In the new white pen,
Lived an old mother pig
And her little pigs ten.
"Play," said the mother.
"We play," said the ten.
So they played all day
In the new white pen.

A Day on the Farm

by Rosalie Macfarlane

Part One: Twins

Jody looked out her bedroom window.
She saw her big brother
coming from the barn.
"Ben," she called.
"Did it happen? Did it happen?"

"Yes," called Ben.
"And there are two of them!
They are in the pen
behind the barn."

Jody ran downstairs.
She saw her brother Jeff
making a kite.
"Jeff," she cried.
"Guess what! It's twins!
Let's go and see them.
I'll race you to the barn."

Jody and Jeff ran
to the sheep pen behind the barn.
They saw a mother sheep
and one baby lamb.
The baby lamb was feeding
from his mother.

"Look at the baby lamb," said Jody.
"He's so small!"

"But look how strong he is,"
 said Jeff.
"He's standing up already."

"Where's the other lamb?" asked Jody.
"He should be here with his mother."

Just then, they heard something.

"It's the other lamb!" said Jody.
"He's bleating for his mother!"

"There he is," said Jeff,
"in the long grass by the fence."

"I think he's hurt!" said Jody.
"I'll run and get Ben."

Jody saw Ben in the field.
He was driving a tractor.

"Ben! Ben!" Jody yelled.
"It's one of the lambs!
He's hurt! Come right away!"

Ben stopped the tractor
and jumped down.
Ben and Jody hurried
back to the fence.
Jeff was waiting there
with the lamb.

Ben looked at the little lamb.
"His leg is caught in the fence.
Be very quiet.
We don't want to frighten him."

The lamb bleated softly.

Gently...gently...
Ben worked to free the lamb.

"His leg is broken," said Ben.

"Can you fix it?" asked Jeff.

"Yes," said Ben,
"but I'll need your help.
First of all,
we'll have to take him
up to the house."

Jody patted the lamb.
"Don't cry," she said.
"We'll take good care of you."

Part Two: Together Again

Jeff, Ben, and Jody
went into the kitchen.

The lamb bleated softly.

"Don't be frightened,"
Jeff said to the lamb.
"We're not going to hurt you."

"Hold him gently," said Ben.
"I want to look at his leg."

"I'll have to put a splint
   on the lamb's leg," said Ben.
"I'll need some sticks and some tape."

"I know what we can use," said Jeff.
"We can use the sticks and tape
   from my kite."

"Good idea," said Ben.

Jeff got two sticks and some tape.

"Hold him still," said Ben.

Jeff and Jody held the lamb.
Ben put a splint on the lamb's leg.

"Is the lamb going to be all right now?"
asked Jody.

"He's very weak," said Ben.
"He needs milk.
We'll have to feed him.

Jody, you come with me.
We'll go and get some milk
from the mother sheep.
Jeff, you stay here
and watch the lamb."
Jody and Ben went to the sheep pen.
They milked the mother sheep.

Jody and Ben took the milk
back to the house.
They fed the milk to the lamb.

"Will he be all right now?"
asked Jody.

"I think so," said Ben.
"He can stand up already."

That afternoon they took the lamb
back to his mother.
He began feeding from her right away.

Jody said, "He's happy now.
He's back with his mother."

"Yes," said Jeff.
"Now the whole family
is together again."

Little Red Ant and Plump White Dove

by Seymour V. Reit, William H. Hooks,
and Betty D. Boegehold

Little Red Ant and Plump White Dove
were talking one day.

Little Red Ant said:

Let's be friends,
Good and true.
You help me
And I'll help you.

Plump White Dove laughed
and said softly:

Coo, coo.
I just can't see
How a little red ant
Can ever help me!

Suddenly a fierce gust of wind
blew Red Ant into the brook.
She called out to White Dove,
"Help! Help! Save me!"

White Dove flew down quickly.
Gently, he lifted Red Ant
out of the water.
Then he set her on a big grey
in the green  .

Little Red Ant looked up
at Plump White Dove and said:

You're a friend,
Good and true.
You helped me,
Now I'll help you.

Plump White Dove laughed again and said:

Coo, coo.
I just can't see
How a little red ant
Can ever help me!

Little Red Ant answered, "Wait and see."

White Dove perched high in the

and began to clean his feathers.

But danger was coming!

The plump dove didn't see the Hunter

with his ⟨bow⟩ and ⟨arrow⟩ ,

who was hiding behind a big ⟨bush⟩ !

The Hunter watched the bird.

Quiet as a  ,

sly as a ,

he crouched behind the .

Smiling, the Hunter said to himself:

Soft, plump Dove,
Fat and white,
I'll have you
For supper tonight.

Little Red Ant began to crawl
toward the Hunter.

She raced

across the grey  ,

through the green ,

under a yellow  ,

over a brown  ,

and
right
up the
Hunter's
leg.

Then she bit his leg very HARD!
"*Yeeeoow! Ouch!*" yelled the Hunter.

He dropped his  and

and began hopping up and down.

Whirrr! Whirrr!
Away flew Plump White Dove,
high into the blue sky,
where he was safe.

Little Red Ant crawled back

over the brown  ,

under the yellow ,

through the green ,

to the big grey  .

Sitting on the big ,
Red Ant waved to White Dove.

High in the sky above her,
White Dove looped and swooped happily.
Then he called:

Coo, coo.
Now I see
How a little red ant
Can help me!

If...

by Ann Ashford

If I picked a little flower up
and put it in a paper cup...

would you smell it?

If my birch tree were afraid at night
and couldn't sleep without a light...

would you bring one?

If my rainbow were to turn all grey
and wouldn't shine at all today. . .

would you paint it?

If I said that I could dance for you,
as hard as that would be to do...

would you watch me?

If I ran backwards up a tree
and called for you to follow me...

would you do it?

If I took an empty midnight train
across the country in the rain...

would you meet me?

If all that I would want to do
would be to sit and talk to you...

would you listen?

Project Manager: Christine Anderson
Editor: Jocelyn Van Huyse
Design and Art Direction: Rob McPhail
Associate Art Directors: Lorraine Tuson and Holly Fisher
Cover Design: Taylor/Levkoe Associates Limited
Cover Illustration: Sharon Matthews
Typesetting: Trigraph Inc.
Printing: The Bryant Press Limited

Acknowledgements

All selections in this book have been written or adapted by John McInnes and John Ryckman, with the exception of the following:

Boris and Morris by Bernard Wiseman: Reprinted by permission of Dodd, Mead and Company, Inc. from MORRIS AND BORIS: THREE STORIES BY BERNARD WISEMAN. Copyright © 1974 by Bernard Wiseman.

Over in the Meadow: Traditional.

A Day on the Farm by Rosalie Macfarlane: Reprinted by permission of the author.

Little Red Ant and Plump White Dove by Seymour V. Reit, William H. Hooks, and Betty D. Boegehold: From WHEN SMALL IS TALL, by Seymour V. Reit, William H. Hooks, and Betty D. Boegehold. Copyright © 1985 by Bank Street College of Education. Illustrations copyright © 1985 by Lynn Munsinger. Reprinted by permission of Random House, Inc.

If... by Ann Ashford: From IF I FOUND A WISTFUL UNICORN. Copyright © 1978 by Ann Ashford. Text reprinted with permission of Peachtree Publishers, Ltd., 494 Armour Circle, N.E., Atlanta, Georgia, 30324.

Illustrations

Brian Boyd: 28-40; Sharon Foster: 11; Darcia Labrosse: 89-95; Mike Martchenko: 12-16, 17-22; Sharon Matthews: 55-64; Lynn Munsinger: 80-88; Karen Patkau: 4; Greg Ruhl: 65-79; Laurie Stein: 26-27; Vlasta Van Kampen: 5-10; Bernard Wiseman: 41-54

Photographs

Jeremy Jones: 4, 23-25, 26-27

7 8 9 0 BP 2 1 0